Singer's Activi[...]

Mr. Funfiddle's Christmas

A Musical Celebration for Kids
by Dennis and Nan Allen

CONTENTS

LILLENAS PUBLISHING COMPANY
Kansas City, MO 64141

THE CHARACTERS
(in order of appearance)

MR. FUNFIDDLE (or MRS. FUNFIDDLE)   May be played by an adult or teen. This character should be very animated and should be able to sing. Solo: "It's Contagious".

JONATHAN PEACEFUL   a boy. Jonathan is a gentleman's gentleman. A very formal, calm sort of chap!

SARAH LOVEGOOD   a girl. Sarah is a sweet homebody-type.

FRANCES JOYHEART   a girl. May be played by an aerobics enthusiast or a gymnast. She's athletic... opposite from Sarah.

JOEY HOPEWELL   a boy. A really cool guy! Preferably a singer, but it's not absolutely necessary.

GIRL #1   a choir member

GIRL #2   a choir member

BOY #1   a choir member

BOY #2   a choir member

OFFICER CASEY   may be played by an adult, a teen, or an older child. He is very official, at least at first. He's just doing his job!

Something to Celebrate!

Words and Music by
DENNIS and NAN ALLEN
Arr. by Dennis Allen

Sun - day best! No - thing's too fan - cy, no - thing's too good_____
you are here! Ev - 'ry - thing's read - y, ev - 'ry - thing's set._____

for our spe - cial guest!
Come and join_____ the fun!

Opt. div.

Repeat 2 times

CODA

The Son of God_____ is born! Cel - e - brate!

Cel - e - brate! And Je - sus is_____ His name! Cel - e - brate!

Cel - e - brate!

We've got some - thing to cel - e - brate! We've got a rea - son to sing!__

_____ It - 'll be some - thing, what_____ an oc - ca - sion, the

birth - day of a King!_____ We've got some - thing to

cel - e - brate! We've got a rea-son to sing!_____

Cel - e-brate!_____ We've got a rea-son to sing!__

It - 'll be some-thing, what__ an oc - ca-sion, the birth - day of a King!__

the birth - day of a King!__

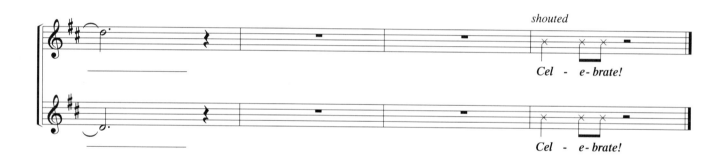

shouted

Cel - e-brate!

Cel - e-brate!

SCENE 1

MR. FUNFIDDLE: *(to the audience)* Oh, hello there. I'm so glad you could join us. Allow me to introduce myself. The name is *Jeremiah Funfiddle and I am a Celebration Specialist. That means, I really know how to throw a party! Tonight, I'm hosting a Christmas celebration and you're invited to all the festivities! *(looking at his clipboard)* Let's see, what's on my list for the party activities tonight! Yes...here it is. We'll sing, we'll play games, we'll have prizes...

(Jonathan Peaceful enters and clears throat)

MR. FUNFIDDLE: Oh, my. What was I thinking? I forgot to introduce you to my co-hosts and hostesses. By all means, may I present...Jonathan Peaceful...

JONATHAN: Good evening.

*Jessica Funfiddle, if played by a female

MR. FUNFIDDLE: Then there's Sarah Lovegood...

SARAH: So glad you could come.

MR. FUNFIDDLE: Frances Joyheart...

FRANCES: Hi, there!

MR. FUNFIDDLE: And Joey Hopewell.

JOEY: Yo!

MR. FUNFIDDLE: These guys ought to be a part of every Christmas celebration. 'Cause they're really the life of the party. Tonight, they've planned a hum-dinger, too, with games and food and...gifts for everyone. That's right– each one of my co-hosts and hostesses will present you with gifts...gifts from the Christmas spirit...Joy, Love, Hope and Peace. Now...

JONATHAN: Excuse me, Mr. Funfiddle.

MR. FUNFIDDLE: Yes, Jonathan.

JONATHAN: Pardon me for saying so, sir, but some of our guests don't look as though they're very happy about being here. *(gestures to the audience)*

MR. FUNFIDDLE: No, they don't, do they?

SARAH: Maybe they haven't gotten the Christmas spirit yet.

MR. FUNFIDDLE: Maybe they haven't, Sarah.

JOEY: *(to the audience)* Hey...it's time you get with the celebratin', dudes.

MR. FUNFIDDLE: Now Joey, maybe they need a little help.

FRANCES: What can we do?

MR. FUNFIDDLE: Well, Frances, maybe we could celebrate for them for a little while...'til they get the hang of it. Ya know, there's something about the Christmas spirit. It's...contagious! *(music begins)* Hey, kids. Let me share a song with you. Maybe later you can join in.

WHAT'S WRONG WITH THIS PICTURE?

In the scene below, see how many things you can find that are wrong.

It's Contagious

Words and Music by
DENNIS and NAN ALLEN
Arr. by Dennis Allen

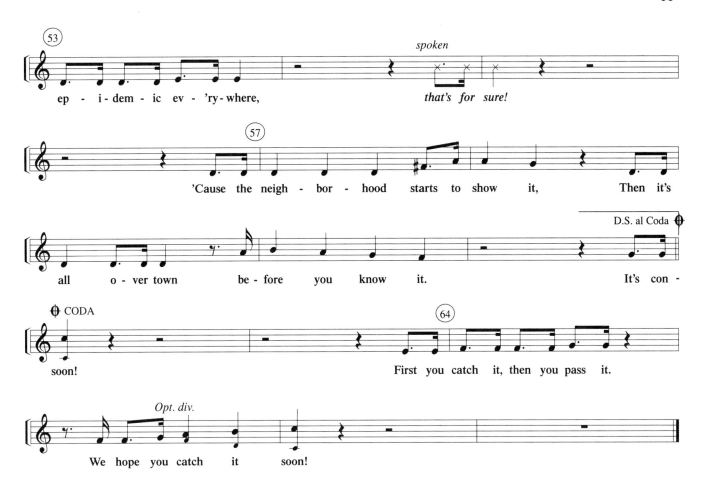

ep - i - dem - ic ev - 'ry - where, *that's for sure!*

'Cause the neigh - bor - hood starts to show it, Then it's

D.S. al Coda

all o - ver town be - fore you know it. It's con -

CODA

soon! First you catch it, then you pass it.

Opt. div.

We hope you catch it soon!

SCENE 2

MR. FUNFIDDLE: *(to the audience)* Hey, are we having fun yet? I see a few smiles out there already and you know what that can lead to, don't you? That's right. Laughter... belly-bustin', breath-takin'...out and out laughter. Remember, it can come on you before you know it. And then there's no telling what'll happen. Oh, look at me...hogging the stage again. Why, I need to let one of my co-hosts come up here and get this party going. Who wants to present the first gift?

FRANCES: Me first!

MR. FUNFIDDLE: Okay. May I present...Frances Joyheart!

(applause)

FRANCES: All right, everybody. Let's play charades.

ALL: Okay...yeah...sounds like fun, etc.

FRANCES: Okay, I've got one. Here goes...

(begins to pantomime)

(Frances: "open book" with hands)

GIRL #1:   It's a song.

(Frances: raises index finger)

BOY #1:   First word.

(Frances: pulls ear lobe)

GIRL #2:   Sounds like...

(Frances: points to a boy #2)

BOY #2:   Sounds like...me?

(Frances: shakes head "no")

BOY #2:   No.

(Frances: points to Boy #2)

GIRL #1:   Sounds like ...dork!

BOY #2:   Hey!

(Frances: shakes head "no")

GIRL #2:   Sounds like...boy!

(Frances: "on the nose")
(Frances continues to mime, etc.)

GIRL #1:   Sounds like boy? Coy! Troy! Toy!

BOY #1:   JOY?

(Frances: "on the nose", raises two fingers)

BOY #2:   Okay, Joy. Next word.

(Frances: tiny word)

GIRL #1:   Little word...and, the, to

(Frances: "on the nose")

GIRL #2:   To...Joy to.

(Frances: tiny word, raises three fingers)

BOY #1:   Third word. Another little word...and, of...the

(Frances: "on the nose")

BOY #2:   Joy to the...

(Frances: raises four fingers: mimes "large round object")

GIRL #1:   Round...earth...ball...big ball...world!

(Frances: "on the nose")

GIRL #1:   Joy to the World!

BOY #1:   I was just about to say that.

GIRL #1:   Oh, please!

FRANCES: "Joy to the World". Very good. A song about joy. Hey, what are some things that bring joy?

BOY #1:   Chocolate.

GIRL #1:   Presents!

BOY #2:   No...dirt bikes!

GIRL #2:   Boys!

FRANCES: Yes. Those things can make you happy, for a little while anyway...but they can't bring you joy.

BOY #1:   Why not?

FRANCES: 'Cause joy doesn't come from things you get...or things that happen around you. It starts inside, in the place that only God can touch. Did you know that there was joy in Bethlehem the night Jesus was born?

GIRL #2:   I'm sure. Everyone's happy when a baby is born.

FRANCES: But that's not why there was joy. You see, Jesus was the gift God sent to the people of earth. But joy was the gift that God sent to their hearts. Hey, I've got a new song about joy. *(music begins)* Here we go, let's sing...

IT'S CONTAGIOUS

Draw a line from the picture to the word that matches it.

SMILE

CHRISTMAS
SPIRIT

LAUGHTER

YAWN

FROWN

FLU

CHICKEN
POX

Joy! Joy! Joy!

with "Joy to the World"

Arr. by Dennis Allen

16

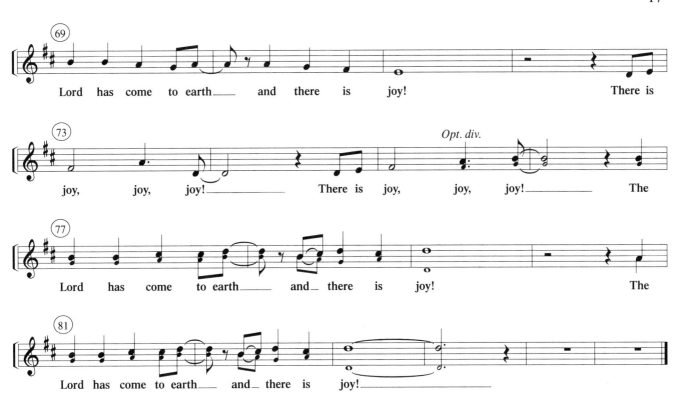

Lord has come to earth___ and there is joy! There is

joy, joy, joy!___ There is joy, joy, joy!___ The

Lord has come to earth___ and___ there is joy! The

Lord has come to earth___ and___ there is joy!___

SCENE 3

(applause)

MR. FUNFIDDLE: Hey, gang, I think they're starting to the get the idea. What do you think?

SARAH: I think they're getting into the spirit, Mr. Funfiddle.

MR. FUNFIDDLE: Me too, Sarah.

SARAH: But I think there are a few people who still need our help. I think my gift might do the trick. My gift is love and I think I know how everybody might get the idea.

MR. FUNFIDDLE: Great, Sarah. What do you want us to do?

SARAH: Let's play musical chairs.

ALL: Oh, cool...great...I love this game.

(NOTE: You may use people from the audience for this game)

SARAH: Okay, I need five people. Good! Now all of you...except one person...get a chair. Line them up. That's right. When the music begins, you start to walk around the chairs. When the music stops, you try to sit in a chair. The one left standing...well, you know what to do, right? This song's about love...and how love is placing our greatest joy in the joy of others. Pay attention to the words. Okay? Here we go.

JOY! JOY! JOY!

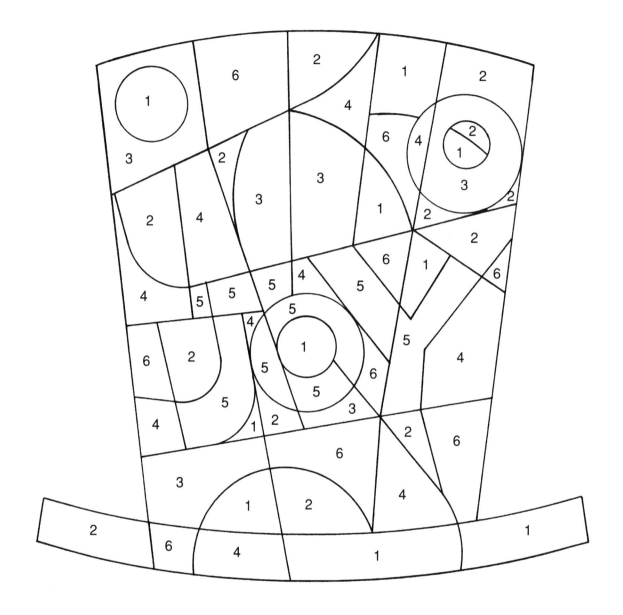

Color Mr. Funfiddle's hat, matching the numbers to the colors.
When you're done, you'll see a gift of the Christmas spirit!

1 = BLUE   4 = ORANGE
2 = GREEN   5 = RED
3 = YELLOW   6 = PURPLE

Love! We're Talkin' Love!

Words and Music by
DENNIS and NAN ALLEN
Arr. by Dennis Allen

1. What would make a Fa - ther send His great - est
2. What would make some - bod - y look be - yond him -

gift to a world that may not rec - og - nize
self to the wants and needs of some - one

Him? Must be some - thing spe - cial,
else?

must be some - thing great. Got - ta be a mir - a - cle,

but all it would take is

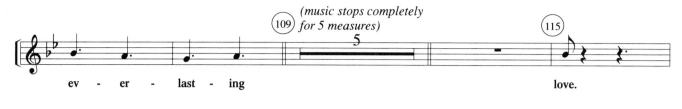

ev - er - last - ing   love.

SCENE 4

MR. FUNFIDDLE:	And the winner is...
SARAH:	The winner is...everybody!
BOY #1:	What?
GIRL #1:	Everybody? How can that be?
BOY #1:	Yeah, I thought the last one standing is the winner.
SARAH:	Maybe in musical chairs, but with the gift of love everybody can give it and get it.
MR. FUNFIDDLE:	Oh, I see. Very good, Sarah. With love, nobody loses, right?
SARAH:	Right! Hey, Mr. Funfiddle. What do you think? *(gestures to audience)* You think they're starting to get the Christmas spirit?
MR. FUNFIDDLE:	Maybe so. I've seen a few smiles...and a few even looked like they wanted to sing.
JOEY:	Yo...Funfiddle. I know how to get 'em to sing.
MR. FUNFIDDLE:	Oh?
JOEY:	Watch this!
MR. FUNFIDDLE:	All right, then. Ladies and gentlemen...Joey Hopewell.

(applause)

JOEY:	*(to the audience)* Hey dudes and dudettes. It's time to jam about hope now. Here's the deal. I sing a line*...then you sing it back. Deal? All right now. This song's about hope and how hope is just waitin' on God to do something cool. Here we go...

(music begins)

*If Joey doesn't sing, alter this dialogue to fit your situation.

LOVE! WE'RE TALKING LOVE!

Below is a list of sentences about love. With your pencil, mark out words that do not appear in the song "Love! We're Talking Love!" What you'll have left will be a good description of love.

LOVE IS . . .

SELFISH   POUTY   PATIENT   A FEELING.

LOVE IS . . .

MEAN   KIND   CHILDISH   RUDE.

LOVE IS A . . .

JOKE   GIFT   PARTY   VIDEO GAME.

LOVE IS SOMETHING . . .

STUPID   MUSHY   SWEET   SPECIAL.

LOVE WOULD SEE . . .

NEEDS OF SOMEBODY ELSE   RED   FLAWS   MISTAKES.

LOVE IS FOR THE . . .

RICH   POOR   PRETTY   WORLD.

Read 1 Corinthians 13.
Find what love is and what love is not.
See if the song says some of the same things about love.

Hope Is

Words and Music by
DENNIS and NAN ALLEN
Arr. by Dennis Allen

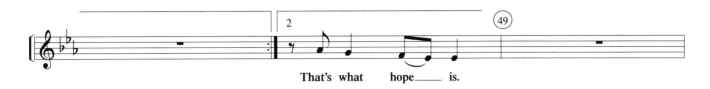

That's what hope___ is.

That's what hope___ is.   That's what hope___ is.

Solo spoken

I'm talk-in' 'bout hope!

SCENE 5

MR. FUNFIDDLE: Let's hear it for Joey Hopewell.

(applause)

JONATHAN: Excuse me, sir.

MR. FUNFIDDLE: Yes, Jonathan?

JONATHAN: Don't mean to be a bother, but refreshments are now being served.

MR. FUNFIDDLE: Oh, great! Let's eat!

(enter Officer Casey)

OFFICER CASEY: I don't think so.

ALL: What? What's going on? etc.

OFFICER CASEY: *(showing ID.)* Officer Casey. 86th Precinct.

MR. FUNFIDDLE: Officer, is there something wrong?

OFFICER CASEY: I'm shuttin' this party down.

SARAH: What? Why?

JOEY: We weren't rockin' too much, were we?

OFFICER CASEY: You're in violation of city ordinance 942...celebrating without a permit.

MR. FUNFIDDLE: Now wait a minute, Officer. I'm a certified Celebration Specialist and I have all the legal clearance I need.

OFFICER CASEY: Not according to our records. *(looking at clipboard)* Says here, you <u>had</u> a permit...but it expired...yesterday!

MR. FUNFIDDLE: Oh, no!

OFFICER CASEY: So...if you'll just pack up all your goodies here and follow me down to the station.

FRANCES: But officer...it's Christmas. You can't ask us to cancel our celebration.

JOEY: *(gestures to the audience)* And some of these people have just gotten into the Christmas spirit. And believe me, it wasn't easy getting them there.

OFFICER CASEY: Tell it to the judge.

SARAH: But officer, you can't do this!

OFFICER CASEY: Look, I'm a peace officer. I'm bound to uphold the law.

JONATHAN: Excuse me, sir. Did you say...peace officer?

MR. FUNFIDDLE: *(has an idea!)* Oh...sure. Jonathan. Why don't you present your gift now? That is, if Officer Casey will allow us.

FRANCES: Yeah, Jonathan. Tell the good officer what <u>real</u> peace is.

OFFICER CASEY: Well...

JONATHAN: Very good. It would be my pleasure. Peace is when your heart is at rest...when it's calm...when it knows that all is well. *(music begins)*

"HOPE IS"

Joey wants to sing! Beside each line of lyrics, write the name of the familiar Christmas song in which that lyric appears. Use your hymnal if you like. Sing a verse of the song that you identify.

1. "... On a cold winter's night that was so deep."_____

2. "... The hopes and fears of all the years are met in thee tonight." _____

3. "... Sleep in heavenly peace."_____

4. "... Let earth receive her King." _____

5. "... Come and behold Him—born the King of angels!"_____

6. "... The stars in the sky look down where He lay,"_____

7. "... This, this is Christ, the King," _____

8. "... In excelsis Deo!" _____

9. "... Joyful, all ye nations, rise;" _____

10. "... Of peace on earth, goodwill to men." _____

Heavenly Peace

with "Silent Night! Holy Night!"

Arr. by Dennis Allen

HEAVENLY PEACE

A code for peace. Decode the message and find out what Isaiah 26:3 says is the way to find the gift of peace. Write the real word underneath the coded word. Read the scripture verse from *The Living Bible*.

"HE WILL KEEP IN

_____

PERFECT PEACE,

_____

ALL THOSE WHO

_____

TRUST IN HIM..."

_____

 = A   =E   =I   =O   =U

SCENE 6

MR. FUNFIDDLE: So officer, what do you think? That's real peace we just sang about. And if you're a peace officer, you wouldn't want to worry about a little thing like an expired permit...would you?

JONATHAN: Don't you think you could allow our celebration to go on under the circumstances, sir?

OFFICER CASEY: Well...

FRANCES: Please...

SARAH: Pretty please...

MR. FUNFIDDLE: I promise I'll come down first thing in the morning and renew my permit.

OFFICER CASEY: No, I'm afraid not. The law's the law!

ALL: Ohhh...man...all that for nothin'...etc.

MR. FUNFIDDLE: Okay, Officer Casey. We understand. Hey guys, let's just get all of this stuff cleaned up.

JOEY: Yo...Funfiddle. You can't give up now. I mean, like...where's your hope, man?

MR. FUNFIDDLE: Hmmm. *(thinking)* Officer, why don't you have a seat right here while we get all of our things together.

OFFICER CASEY: Oh...all right...but just for a minute.

(Officer Casey sits in a chair at center stage)

MR. FUNFIDDLE: Have a cookie, Officer. Make yourself at home.

OFFICER CASEY: Well...if you insist.

MR. FUNFIDDLE: *(music begins)* Hey, kids. Come here for a second.

(Mr. Funfiddle whispers something to the hosts)
(during the song, the hosts work on Officer Casey's smile. They put a party hat on him, drape him with streamers, give him party favors, etc.)
(Officer Casey "gets in the spirit" and even begins to sing and sneezes at the end of the song)

It's Contagious
Reprise

Words and Music by
DENNIS and NAN ALLEN
Arr. by Dennis Allen

Mr. Funfiddle and choir

all o - ver you be - fore you know it. It's con-

ta - gious. The Christ-mas spir - it is con - ta - gious.

We can pass it a-long in word and song. It's con-

ta - gious. The Christ-mas spir - it is con - ta - gious.

Opt. div.

And we hope you catch it soon!

SCENE 7

OFFICER CASEY:	Ah-choo! Excuse me. I must be allergic to something.
FRANCES:	What do you say, Officer? Can we have our party?
OFFICER:	But it says right here that your permit must be renewed on the...*(looking at permit)* next business day....<u>after</u> it expires! Well, how 'bout that? I never noticed that.
SARAH:	What does that mean?
OFFICER:	It means you're still legal...for three more hours!
MR. FUNFIDDLE:	Long enough for us to finish our party!

JOEY: Cool!

JONATHAN: Very good, sir.

OFFICER CASEY: Hey, I guess the Christmas spirit <u>is</u> contagious. I think you gave it to me.

SARAH: Well, actually, we don't <u>give</u> the Christmas spirit.

OFFICER CASEY: No? But I thought you said it was contagious.

SARAH: It is, but the Christmas spirit is a gift that first comes from God. All we do is let it kind of overflow in us...and then other people see it and want it, too.

MR. FUNFIDDLE: And that <u>first</u> gift then gives you <u>more</u> gifts...like joy, for instance.

FRANCES: ...which is praise to God...deep down in your heart.

MR. FUNFIDDLE: And love...

SARAH: ...which is getting your greatest joy in seeing joy in others.

JOEY: And hope. That's hangin' on and lookin' for the next cool thing God's gonna do.

JONATHAN: And of course, peace...sir. It's a calm that happens inside you.

MR. FUNFIDDLE: That's right. The Christmas spirit starts with a silent celebration that goes on inside your heart when Jesus has been invited there first. *(music begins)* See, He's really the only One who can give us the gifts of Joy, Love, Hope, and Peace anyway.

The Pleasure of Your Company

with "Thou Didst Leave Thy Throne"

Arr. by Dennis Allen

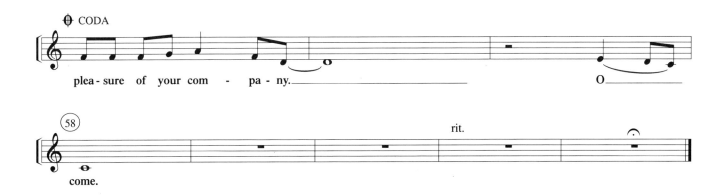

plea - sure of your com - pa - ny.

come.

rit.

SCENE 8

MR. FUNFIDDLE: *(to audience)* Well, as a certified Celebration Specialist, I can say without question that we had a great Christmas party! There was music, and games, and we had a few surprises, too! But more than that, it looks as though some of <u>you</u> actually caught the Christmas spirit. Now all we ask you to do is to pass it along to somebody else. 'Cause I think you'll agree...we've got something to celebrate!

THE PLEASURE OF YOUR COMPANY

Company's coming and you need to show him where he will stay. Start at the door and follow the maze with your pencil until you find the right way to the guest room.

Imagine this house being your life. Imagine Jesus being the company that's coming to stay with you. Imagine His room being the center of the maze. Christ really wants to come into your life. Please let Him in . . . and let Him stay at the center of your heart!

GUEST ROOM

START

Memorize Revelation 3:20.

Something to Celebrate

Finale

Arr. by Dennis Allen

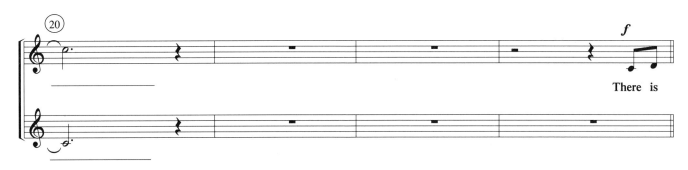

joy,   joy,   joy! _____   There is   joy,   joy,   joy! _____   The

*"Joy! Joy! Joy!" (Allen)

Lord   has   come   to earth ___   and   there   is   joy!   There is

joy,   joy,   joy! _____   There is   joy,   joy,   joy! _____   The

Opt. div.

Lord   has   come   to earth ___   and __ there   is   joy! _____

**"O Come, All Ye Faithful" (Wade)

O   come,   all   ye   faith - ful,

It-'ll be some-thing, what__ an oc - ca-sion, the birth - day of a King!_

Part I

_____ We've got some-thing to cel - e - brate!

Optional Part II **f**

Cel - e - brate!_

We've got a rea-son to sing!_____ It - 'll be some-thing, what_

_____ We've got a rea-son to sing!____

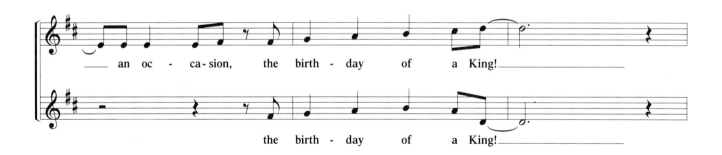

__ an oc - ca-sion, the birth - day of a King!_____

the birth - day of a King!_____

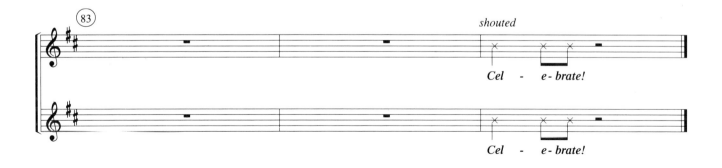

shouted

Cel - e - brate!

Cel - e - brate!